BEAUTIFUL BOTANICALS

A COLORING BOOK OF LOVELY FLOWERS AND GARDENS

chartwell
books

Let your creativity blossom and grow!

Be inspired by nature and start your coloring journey today!

Imagine spending a delightful day roaming around a lovely botanical garden where the flowers are blooming, and the sun is shining. With *Beautiful Botanicals*, you can both enjoy and color the gorgeous plants and foliage you would find in a garden, whether you're at home indoors or traveling.

Inside this coloring book you'll find interesting leaves, blooming flowers, and a variety of other botanical plants. Many of these plants are used for their medicinal or therapeutic properties and scents. Chamomile, ginseng, dandelion root, and echinacea are all common botanicals used in supplements, teas, and essential oils. Some of them are also inside these pages just waiting for you to color!

Take a break from your busy life to color these amazing patterns and designs. Coloring is a great mindfulness activity to help reduce stress and anxiety. It's also a way to express and nurture your creativity, even if you have no previous artistic experience.

Relax your mind and feel your stress fade away when coloring these lovely flowers and gardens. You can use natural and neutral colors or bright primary colors to add your own creative spin to these botanicals.

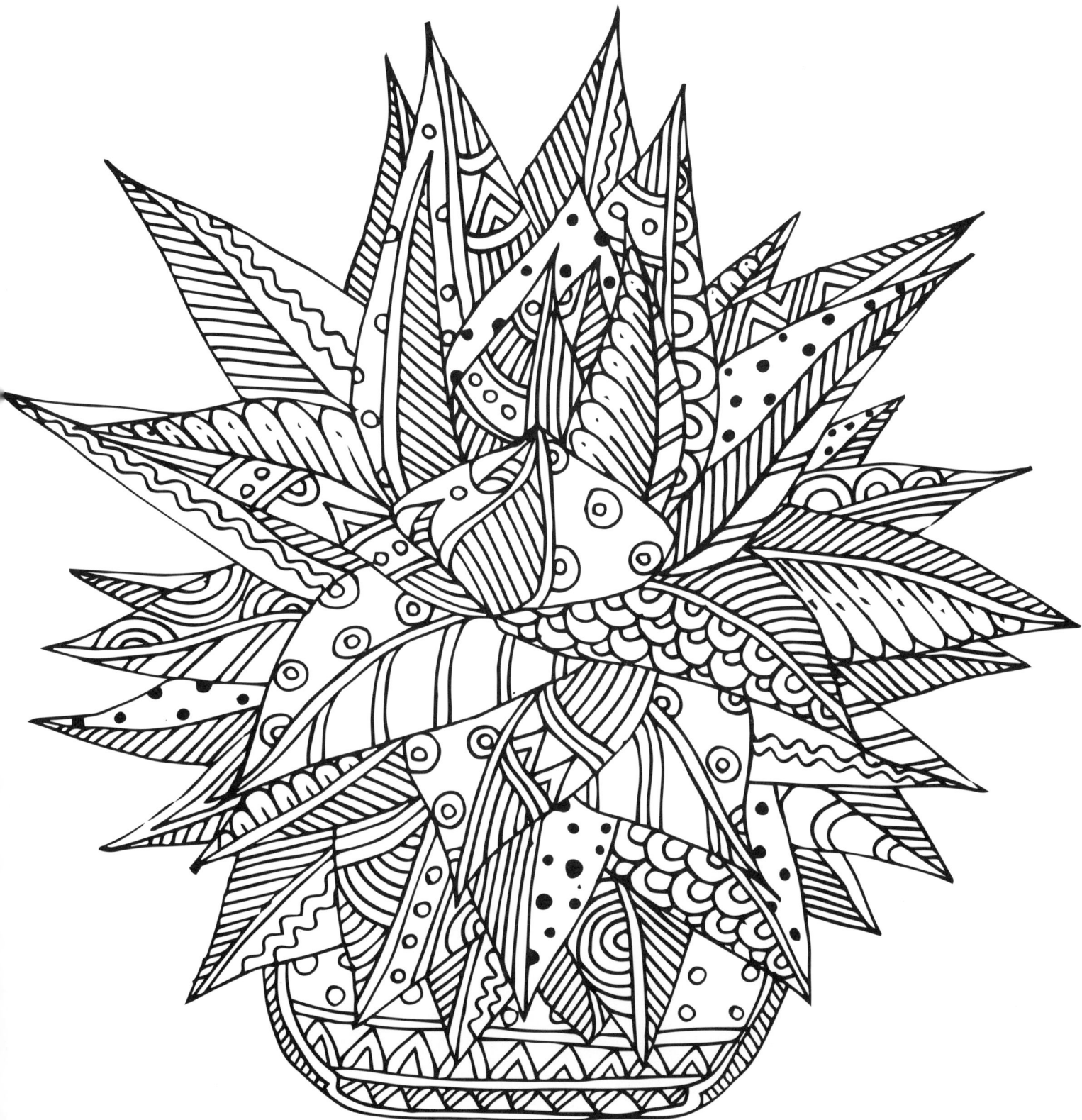

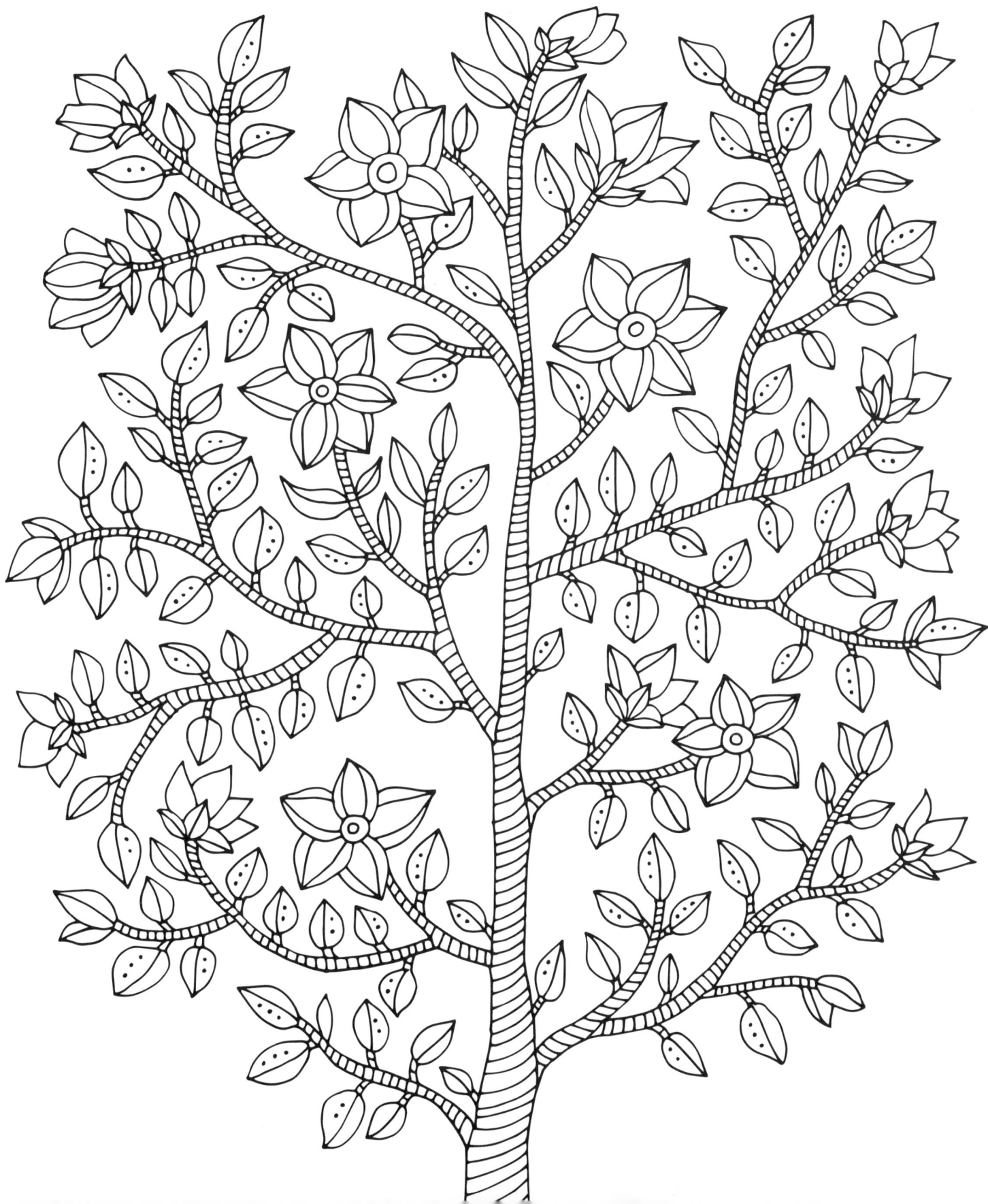

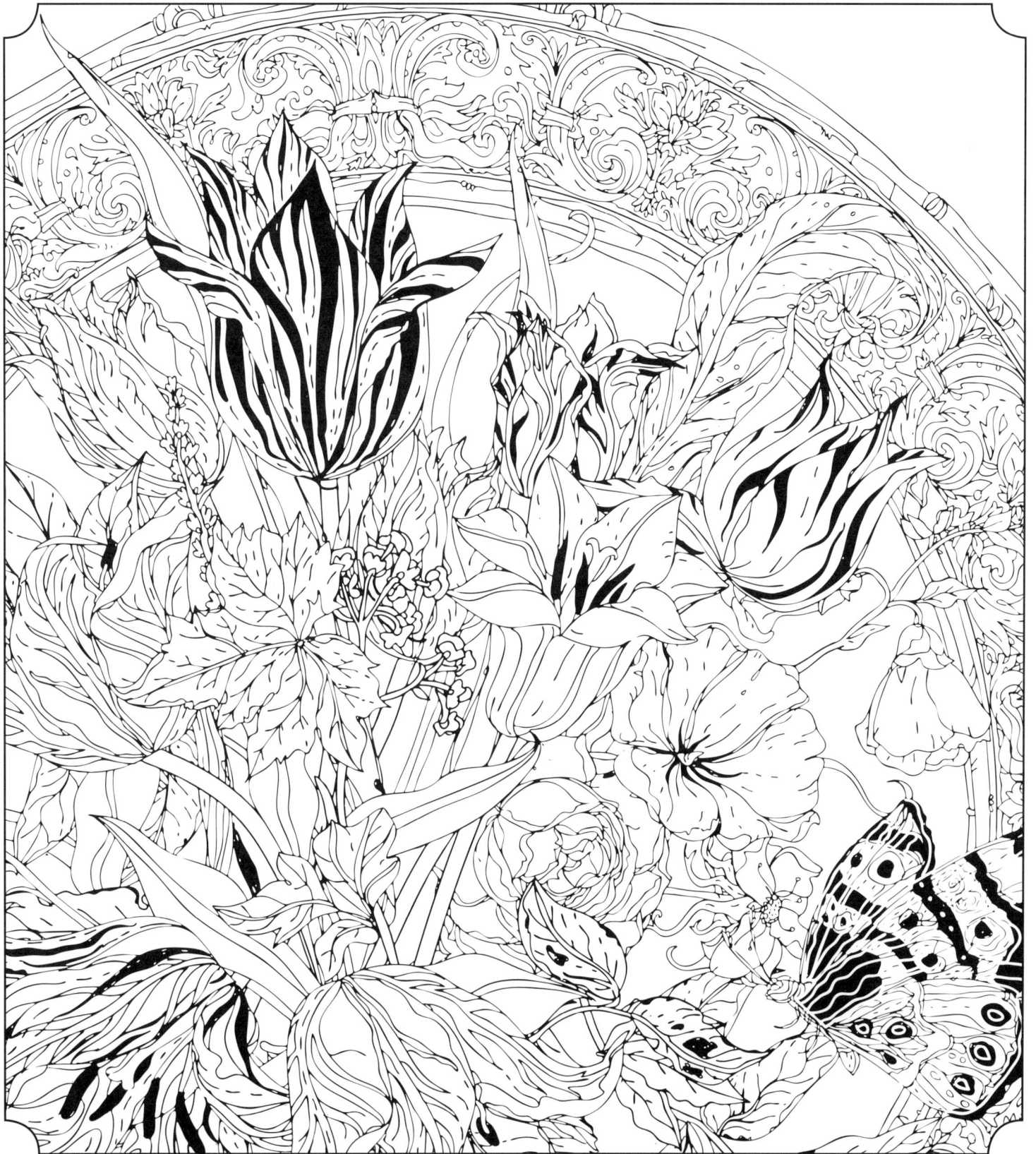

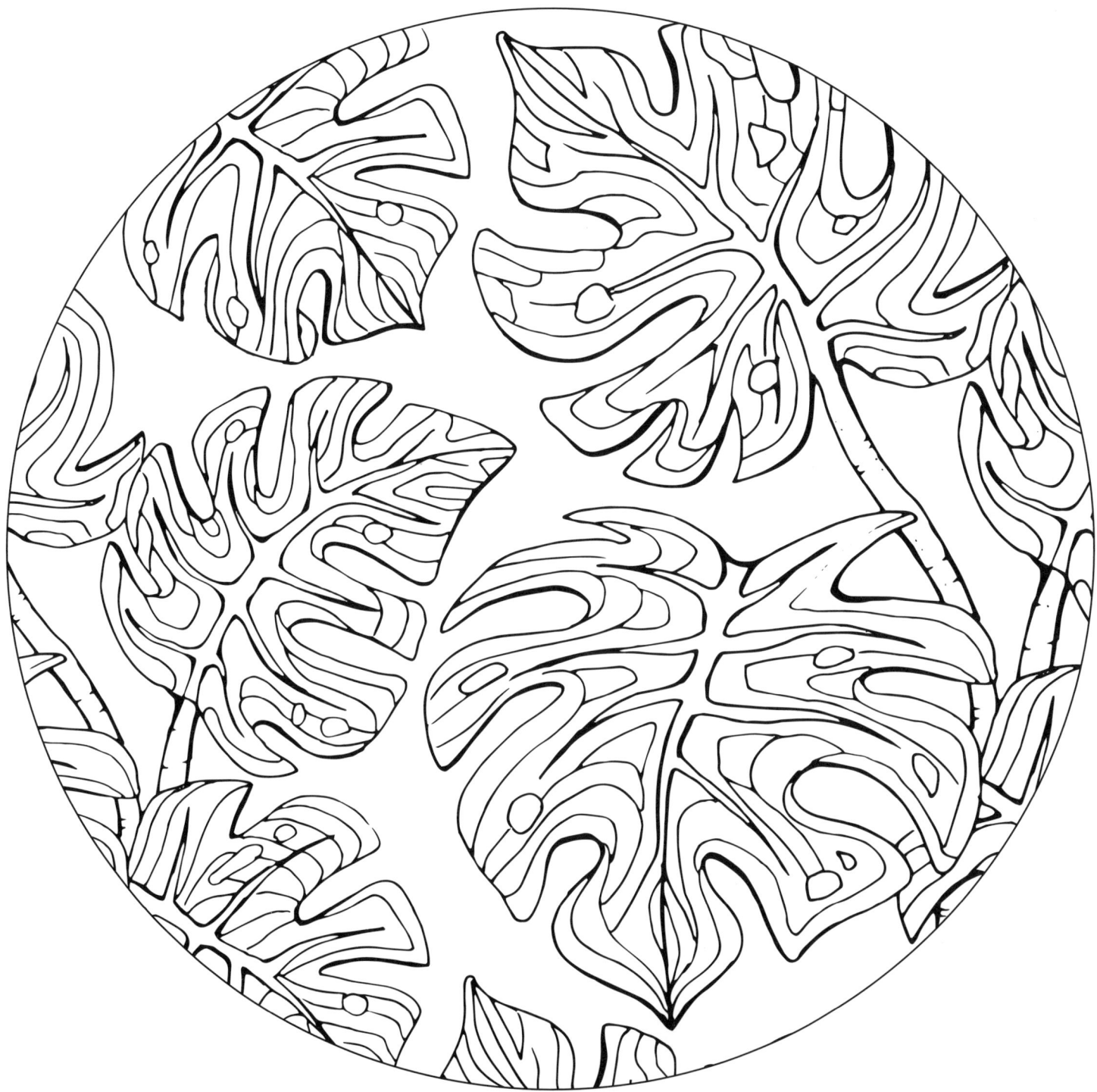

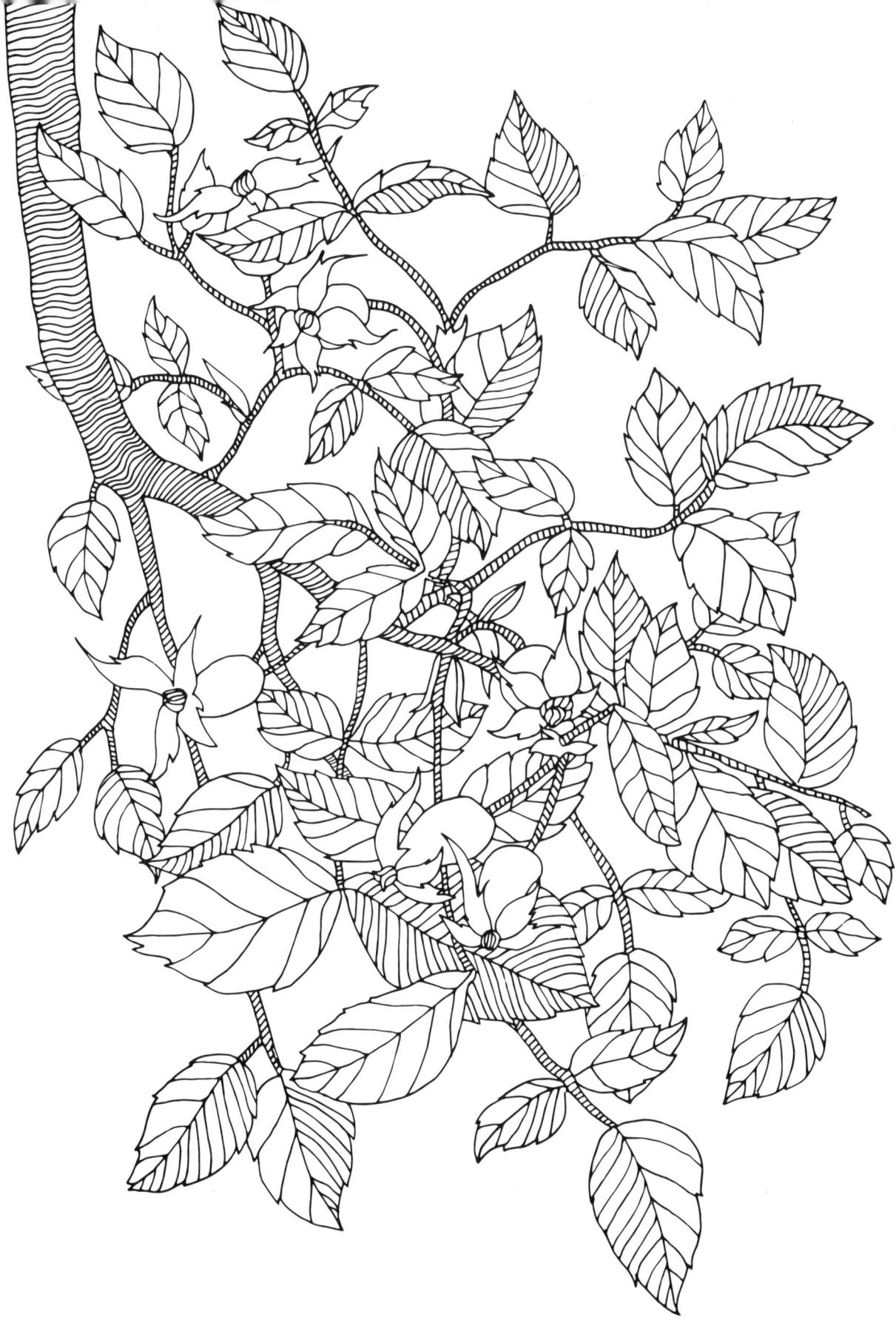

Quarto

© 2024 Quarto Publishing Group USA Inc.

This edition published in 2024 by Chartwell Books,
an imprint of The Quarto Group
142 West 36th Street, 4th Floor
New York, NY 10018 USA
T (212) 779-4972 F (212) 779-6058
www.Quarto.com

10 9 8 7 6 5 4 3 2 1

Chartwell titles are also available at discount for retail, wholesale, promotional, and bulk purchase. For details, contact the Special Sales Manager by email at specialsales@quarto.com or by mail at The Quarto Group, Attn: Special Sales Manager, 100 Cummings Center Suite 265D, Beverly, MA 01915, USA.

ISBN: 978-0-7858-4506-5

Publisher: Wendy Friedman
Senior Managing Editor: Meredith Mennitt
Designer: Alana Ward
Editor: Cathy Davis
Image credits: Shutterstock

Printed in China